CW00558731

中国国家汉办赠送
Donated by Hanban,China

Wise Men Talking Series

SUN ZI
孙子说 Says

蔡希勤 编注

□ 责任编辑 **韩晖**
□ 翻译 **王琴 姜防震**
□ 绘图 **李士伋**

华语教学出版社
SINOLINGUA

First Edition   2006

Second Printing 2007

Third Printing   2009

ISBN 978-7-80200-214-2

Copyright 2006 by Sinolingua

Published by Sinolingua

24 Baiwanzhuang Road, Beijing 100037, China

Tel: (86) 10-68320585

Fax: (86) 10-68326333

http://www.sinolingua.com.cn

E-mail: hyjx@sinolingua.com.cn

Printed by Beijing Foreign Languages Printing House

Distributed by China International Book Trading Corporation

35 Chegongzhuang Xilu, P. O. Box 399

Beijing 100044, China

Printed in the People's Republic of China

老人家说
Wise Men Talking

俗曰:"不听老人言,吃亏在眼前。"

老人家走的路多,吃的饭多,看的书多,经的事多,享的福多,受的罪多,可谓见多识广,有丰富的生活经验,老人家说的话多是经验之谈,后生小子不可不听也。

在中国历史上,春秋战国时期是中国古代思想高度发展的时期,那个时候诸子并起,百家争鸣,出现了很多"子"字辈的老人家,他们有道家、儒家、墨家、名家、法家、兵家、阴阳家,多不胜数,车载斗量,一时星河灿烂。

后来各家各派的代表曾先后聚集于齐国稷下学宫,齐宣王是个开明的诸侯王,因纳无盐丑女钟离春为后而名声大噪,对各国来讲学的专家学者不问来路一律管吃管住,享受政府津贴,对愿留下来做官的,授之以客卿,造巨室,付万钟。对不愿做官的,也给予"不治事而议论"之特殊待遇。果然这些人各为其主,各为其派,百家争鸣,百花齐放,设坛辩论,著书立说:有的说仁,有的说义,有的说无为,有的说逍遥,有的说非攻,有的说谋攻,有的说性善,有的说性恶,有的说亲非亲,有的说马非马,知彼知已,仁者无敌……留下了很多光辉灿烂的学术经典。

可惜好景不长,秦始皇时丞相李斯递话说"焚书坑儒",结果除秦记、医药、卜筮、种树书外,民间所藏诗、书及百家典籍一把火烧个精光。到西汉武帝时,董仲舒又上了个折子,提出"罢黜百家,独尊儒术",从此,儒学成了正统,"黄老、刑名百家之言"成为邪说。

"有德者必有言",儒学以外的各家各派虽屡被扫荡,却不断变幻着生存方式以求不灭,并为我们保存下了十分丰富的经典著作。在这些经典里,先哲们留下了很多充满智慧和哲理的、至今仍然熠熠发光的至理名言,我们将这些各家各派的老人家的"金玉良言"编辑成这套《老人家说》丛书,加以注释并译成英文,采取汉英对照出版,以飨海内外有心有意于中国传统文化的广大读者。

As the saying goes, "If an old dog barks, he gives counsel. "

Old men, who walk more roads, eat more rice, read more books, have more experiences, enjoy more happiness, and endure more sufferings, are experienced and knowledgeable, with rich life experience. Thus, what they say is mostly wise counsel, and young people should listen to them.

The Spring and Autumn (722 – 481 BC) and War-ring States (475 – 221 BC) periods of Chinese history were a golden age for ancient Chinese thought. In those periods, various schools of thought, together with many sages whose names bore the honorific suffix "Zi", e-merged and contended, including the Taoist school, Confucian school, Mohist school, school of Logicians, Legalist school, Military school and Yin-Yang school. Numerous and well known, these schools of thought were as brilliant as the Milky Way.

Later representatives of these schools of thought flocked to the Jixia Academy of the State of Qi. Duke Xuan of Qi was an enlightened ruler, famous for making an ugly but brilliant woman his empress. The duke pro-vided board and lodging, as well as government subsi-dies for experts and scholars coming to give lectures, and never inquired about their backgrounds. For those willing to hold official positions, the duke appointed them guest officials, built mansions for them and paid them high salaries. Those unwilling to take up official posts were kept on as advisors. This was an era when "one hundred schools of thought contended and a hundred flowers blossomed." The scholars debated in forums, and wrote books to expound their doctrines: Some preached benevolence; some, righteousness; some, inaction; some, absolute freedom; some, aversion to offensive war; some, attack by stratagem; some, the goodness of man's nature; some, the evil nature of man. Some said that relatives were not relatives; some said that horses were not horses; some urged the importance of knowing oneself and one's enemy; some said that benevolence knew no enemy... And they left behind many splendid classic works of scholarship.

Unfortunately, this situation did not last long. When Qin Shihuang (reigned 221 – 206 BC) united all the states of China, and ruled as the First Emperor, his prime minister, Li Si, ordered that all books except those on medicine, fortune telling and tree planting be burned. So, all poetry collections and the classics of the various schools of thought were destroyed. Emperor Wu (reigned 140 – 88 BC) of the Western Han Dynasty made Confucianism the orthodox doctrine of the state, while other schools of thought, including the Taoist and Legalist schools, were deemed heretical.

These other schools, however, managed to survive, and an abundance of their classical works have been handed down to us. These classical works contain many wise sayings and profound insights into philosophical theory which are still worthy of study today. We have compiled these nuggets of wisdom uttered by old men of the various ancient schools of thought into this series Wise Men Talking, and added explanatory notes and English translation for the benefit of both Chinese and overseas readers fond of traditional Chinese culture.

目录
CONTENTS

兵闻拙速〔10〕

While we have heard of blundering when seeking swift decisions in war...

兵无常势，水无常形〔12〕

There is no fixed pattern in the use of war tactics, just as there is no constant form in the flow of water.

兵以诈立，以利动〔14〕

War is a game of deception.

兵者，诡道也〔16〕

War is a game of deception.

兵者，国之大事〔18〕

War is a question of vital importance to the state...

兵之情主速〔20〕

In war, speed is the overriding consideration.

兵之所加，如以碫投卵者〔22〕

By staying clear of the enemy's strong points and striking at his weak points, you will be able to...

不尽知用兵之害者〔24〕

Those who are not fully aware of the harm in waging war...

不可胜者，守也〔26〕

Invulnerability lies in defense…

不知军之不可以进而谓之进〔28〕

He arbitrarily orders his army to advance or retreat when in

fact it should not…

不知三军之权而同三军之任〔30〕

He interferes with the officers' command, unaware of the

principle that an army should adopt different…

不知三军之事而同三军之政〔32〕

He interferes with the administration of the army when he is

ignorant of its internal affairs...

C

出其所不趋，趋其所不意〔34〕

Appear at places which the enemy cannot reinforce and where

he least expects you.

D

地形者，兵之助也〔36〕

Advantageous terrain can be a natural ally in battle.

斗众如斗寡〔38〕

There is no difference between commanding a large army and

a small one.

F

发火有时，起火有日〔40〕

There is appropriate weather and appropriate days to start a
fire.

凡军必知有五火之变〔42〕

The army must know which of the five kinds of fire attack to
use according to the different situations...

凡军好高而恶下〔44〕

Generally speaking, a maneuvering army prefers high, dry
ground to low, wet ground.

凡先处战地而待敌者佚〔46〕

Generally speaking, he who first occupies the battlefield and
awaits his enemy is rested and prepared...

凡用兵之法，全国为上，破国次之〔48〕

Generally in war, the best policy is to take the enemy state
whole and intact; to destroy it is second-best.

凡战者，以正合，以奇胜〔50〕

Generally in battle, use normal and regular methods to engage
the enemy, and use unusual and unexpected methods to

achieve victory.

反间者，因其敌间而用之〔52〕

An internal agent, or double agent, is an enemy spy whom you employ.

方马埋轮，未足恃也〔54〕

It is unlikely that you can make soldiers fight to the end just by tethering the horses and burying the chariot wheels.

非利不动，非得不用〔56〕

Do not go into battle if it is not in the interest of the state.

非圣智不能用间〔58〕

He who lacks wisdom cannot use agents...

纷纷纭纭，斗乱而不可乱〔60〕

Amidst the chaos of men and horses locked in battle beneath waving banners, there must be no disorder in command.

夫兵形像水〔62〕

Now the law governing military operations is as that governing the flow of water...

夫钝兵挫锐〔64〕

When your weapons are blunted and your morale dampened...

夫未战而庙算胜者，得算多也〔66〕

He who makes a full assessment of the situation at the prewar council meeting in the temple is more likely to win.

夫吴人与越人相恶也〔68〕

The people of Wu and the people of Yue hate each other.

G

攻其无备，出其不意〔70〕

Attack when the enemy is least prepared. Take action when he least expects you.

攻而必取者，攻其所不守也〔72〕

That you are certain to take what you attack is because you attack a place the enemy cannot protect.

挂形者，敌无备，出而胜之〔74〕

The nature of this terrain gua, which enmeshes, is such that if the enemy is unprepared and you go out to engage him...

国之贫于师者远输〔76〕

When a country is impoverished by military operations, it is because of the long-distance transportation involved.

H

厚而不能使，爱而不能令〔78〕

If a commander indulges his troops to the point at which he

cannot use them. . .

火发上风，无攻下风〔80〕

If fire is set upwind, do not attack from downwind.

J

激水之疾，至于漂石者，势也〔82〕

Torrential water can move boulders because of its momentum.

计利以听，乃为之势〔84〕

Having accepted my assessment of the relative advantages

and disadvantages. . .

间事未发，而先闻者〔86〕

If plans relating to secret operations are prematurely divulged. . .

将有五危〔88〕

There are five weaknesses of character for a commander.

校之以计，而索其情〔90〕

When assessing the outcome of a war, compare the two

sides. . .

进而不可御者，冲其虚也〔92〕

His advance is irresistible because he plunges into his enemy's weak position.

经之以五事〔94〕

To assess the outcome of a war, examine and compare the two sides in terms of the following five factors.

九地之变〔96〕

The different handling of the nine kinds of regions...

绝地无留〔98〕

The army should not linger in enemy-occupied areas...

军无辎重则亡〔100〕

An army without its equipment, food and fodder, and material reserves cannot survive.

K

客绝水而来〔102〕

When the advancing enemy is crossing a river...

Q

其疾如风，其徐如林〔104〕

When the army advances, it is as swift as the wind; when it is immobile, as still as the forest.

其用战也，胜久则钝兵挫锐〔106〕

In a war involving a huge army, the main objective should be quick victory.

三军可夺气，将军可夺心〔108〕

An entire army can be demoralized and its general deprived of his presence of mind.

三军之事，莫亲于间〔110〕

Of all those in the army close to the commander, nobody is more intimate than the agent.

三军之众，可使必受敌而无败者〔112〕

The army is able to withstand the onslaught of the enemy forces.

善攻者，敌不知其所守〔114〕

Against the expert in attack, the enemy does not know where to defend. . .

善守者，藏于九地之下〔116〕

He who is skilled in defense positions his forces in places as safe and inaccessible as in the depths of the Earth. . .

善用兵者，譬如率然〔118〕

Those who are skilled in employing troops are like the snake found on Mount Chang.

善用兵者，屈人之兵而非战也〔120〕
He who is skilled in war subdues the enemy without fighting.

善用兵者，修道而保法〔122〕
He who is skilled in deploying troops seeks victory by
cultivating the Tao and strengthening rules and regulations. . .

善用兵者，役不再籍〔124〕
Those adept at waging war do not require a second conscription
or replenishment of provisions from the home country.

善战人之势，如转圆石于千仞之山者〔126〕
He who is skilful in turning the situation to his advantage can
send his men into battle as he would roll logs or rocks···

善战者，立于不败之地〔128〕
He who is skilled in deploying troops puts himself in a
position in which he cannot be defeated. . .

善战者，其势险，其节短〔130〕
When launching an offensive, a good commander creates a
good posture . . .

善战者，求之于势〔132〕
One who is skilled at directing war always tries to turn the

situation to his advantage. . .

上兵伐谋〔134〕

The best policy in war is to thwart the enemy's strategy.

胜兵先胜而后求战〔136〕

A victorious army will not engage the enemy unless it is

assured of the necessary conditions for victory. . .

胜者之战，若决积水于千仞之溪〔138〕

A victorious army goes into battle with the force of an

onrushing torrent, which, when suddenly released. . .

始如处女，敌人开户〔140〕

Before action starts, appear as shy as a maiden, and the

enemy will relax his vigilance and leave his door open.

视卒如婴儿〔142〕

Because the commander cares for his soldiers as if they were

his children, they will follow him through the greatest

dangers.

T

通形者，先居高阳〔144〕

On a terrain of tong which is accessible, he who first occupies

the sunny, high ground . . .

投之亡地然后存〔146〕

Only when you throw the troops into a life-and-death situation will they fight to survive.

途有所不由，军有所不击〔148〕

There are roads the commander should not take, armies he should not attack...

W

为客之道〔150〕

The general rule of operation for an invading force is that...

惟明君贤将，能以上智为间者〔152〕

Only the enlightened king and wise commander who are capable of using the most intelligent people as agents...

我欲战，敌虽高垒深沟〔154〕

When we want to start battle, the enemy cannot but leave his position to engage us...

无所不备，则无所不寡〔156〕

An army which has to prepare against the enemy everywhere is bound to be weak everywhere.

无邀正正之旗〔158〕

Do not intercept an enemy whose banners are in perfect array.

先知者，不可取于鬼神〔160〕

Foreknowledge cannot be obtained from ghosts or spirits. . .

小敌之坚，大敌之擒也〔162〕

No matter how stubbornly a small force may fight, it must in the end succumb to greater strength, and fall captive to it.

行火必有因〔164〕

To launch a fire attack, certain conditions are required.

形人而我无形〔166〕

If we are able to determine the enemy's disposition while concealing our own. . .

Y

以火佐攻者明〔168〕

Using fire to assist in attacks can produce notable results. . .

以近待远，以佚待劳〔170〕

Being close to the battlefield, he awaits an enemy coming from afar. . .

以治待乱，以静待哗〔172〕

In good order, he awaits a disorderly enemy. . .

用兵之法，十则围之〔174〕

The art of using troops is: when you outnumber the enemy

ten to one, surround him.

用兵之法，无恃其不来〔176〕

It is a rule in war that you must not count on the enemy not

coming...

用间有五〔178〕

There are five kinds of spies...

Z

战道必胜〔180〕

If the way of war guarantees you victory...

战势不过奇正〔182〕

In military tactics, there are only two types of operation: qi

(unusual and unexpected attack) and zheng...

支形者，敌虽利我，我无出也〔184〕

On the kind of terrain zhi which is disadvantageous to both

sides, even if the enemy tempts you...

知彼知己，胜乃不殆〔186〕

Know your enemy and know yourself, and victory will not be

in question...

知彼知己，百战不殆〔188〕

Know your enemy and know yourself, and you can fight a

14

hundred battles without peril.

知兵之将，民之司命〔190〕

The commander who knows how to conduct a war is the
arbiter of the people's fate...

知兵者，动而不迷〔192〕

Those who are well versed in warfare are never bewildered
when they take action...

知可以战与不可以战者胜〔194〕

The side which knows when to fight and when not to will win...

智将务食于敌〔196〕

A wise general does his best to feed his troops on the
enemy's grain.

智者之虑，必杂于利害〔198〕

In his deliberations, the wise commander will take into
account both the favorable and the unfavorable factors.

主不可以怒而兴师〔200〕

The king should not start a war simply out of anger...

15

孙子说

孙子,姓孙名武,字长卿。春秋末齐国人,本田姓,其祖父田书因伐莒功大,齐景公二十五年"赐姓孙",此时孙武22岁,后人也称孙武子。

齐景公三十三年,孙武奔吴,为吴王阖庐作《兵法》十三篇,试之以宫中美人,甚善,于是"吴王知孙子能用兵,卒以为将。西破强楚,入郢,北威齐、晋,显名诸侯"。

《兵法》十三篇,被古今军事家们奉为圭臬,曹操曰:"吾观兵书战策多矣,孙武所著深矣。"

孙子主张"谋攻"。名言曰:"知彼知己,百战不殆。""不战而屈人之兵,善之善者也。""攻其无备,出其不意。""善战者,致人而不致于人。""善攻者,动于九天之上;善守者,藏于九地之下。"

Sun Zi's name was Sun Wu with the courtesy name Changqing. He was a native of the State of Qi at late Spring and Autumn Period. Originally his family name was Tian. As his grandfather Tian Shu rendered outstanding service in leading an expedition against the State of Ju〔resent Ju County in Shandong Province〕, he was bestowed the surname Sun in the 25th year under the reign of Qi Jinggong. At that time, Sun Wu was 22 years old, and thus people of later generations also call him Sun Wu Zi.

In the 33rd year under the reign of Qi Jinggong, Sun Wu went to the State of Wu, and wrote for He Lu, King of Wu, the Art of War embodying 13 chapters. He tried it on beauties of the imperial palace, and found it quite useful. And then "the King of Wu knew that Sun Zi was skilled in employing troops and made him his gene r-al. In the west Sun Zi defeated the strong State of Chu and entered its capital Ying; and in the north he domineered over the states of Qi and Jin, and made his name among dukes."

The 13-chapter Art of War has been regarded as the criterion by ancient and modern strategists. Cao Cao said, "The books on the art of war I read are so many, but that of Sun Wu is the most profound."

Sun Zi advocated to "attack by stratagem." His famous sayings include: "Know your enemy and know yourself, and you can fight a hundred battles without peril." "To break the enemy's resistance without fighting is the wisest thing." "Attack when the enemy is least prepared. Take action when he least expects you." "Those skilled in war move the enemy rather than allow themselves to be moved by him." "He who is skilled in attack strikes as from the highest reaches of Heaven, whereas he who is skilled in defense positions his forces in places as safe and inaccessible as in the depths of the Earth."

百战百胜，非善之善者也

To fight a hundred battles and win each and every one of them is not the wisest thing to do.

百战百胜，非善之善者也；不战而屈人之兵，善之善者也。

《孙子·谋攻篇》

To fight a hundred battles and win each and every one of them is not the wisest thing to do. To break the enemy's resistance without fighting is the wisest thing.

【注释】

善之善：好中最好的。**不战而屈人之兵**：不经交战就能使敌人屈服。

孙子认为，不战而屈人之兵，多的是王者之气，靠的是天道民心。而以战屈人之兵则是以杀人掠地的霸气。这就是孙子主张的"全军为上，破军次之。"

【译文】

百战百胜，还并不是好中最好的，不经交战而能使敌人屈服的才是好中最好的。

避其锐气，击其惰归

Avoid the enemy when the latter's spirit is high, and strike when his spirit is drained.

避其锐气，击其惰归，此治气者也。

《孙子·军争篇》

Avoid the enemy when the latter's spirit is high, and strike when his spirit is drained.

【注释】

惰归：惰，怠惰。《荀子·非十二子》："佚而不惰，劳而不侵。"归，归去，回家。

孙子认为军队初战时，士气很旺盛，经过一段时间僵持不下之后，就逐渐怠惰，到了后来，士卒就会气竭思归。故说"朝气锐，昼气惰，暮气归"。

【译文】

避开敌人初战时的锐气，等到敌人怠惰疲惫时再果断出击，这是掌握军队士气的方法。

兵贵胜，不贵久

What is important in war is quick victory, not prolonged operations.

兵贵胜，不贵久。

《孙子·作战篇》

What is important in war is quick victory, not prolonged operations.

【注释】

兵贵胜：用兵作战以能取得胜利为可贵。

孙子主张用兵作战贵胜不贵久，久则对国家财力、人力和物力的消耗过大，所以他说："夫兵久而国利者，未之有也。"

【译文】

用兵作战以取胜为贵，不以拖延持久为能。

兵怒而相迎，久而不合

When an enemy confronts you angrily for a long time without either joining battle or retreating...

兵怒而相迎，久而不合，又不相去，必谨察之。

《孙子·行军篇》

When an enemy confronts you angrily for a long time without either joining battle or retreating, then you must watch him with the utmost care.

【注释】

久而不合：长时间不交战。合，古代称交战曰合。《史记·萧相国世家》："臣等身披坚执锐，多者百余战，少者数十合。"

【译文】

敌军盛怒而来，剑拔弩张，互相对峙，却长时间既不交锋，也不撤离，对这种反常情况必须谨慎观察敌军动态，伺机采取行动。

兵闻拙速

While we have heard of blundering when seeking swift decisions in war. . .

兵闻拙速，未睹巧之久也。

《孙子·作战篇》

While we have heard of blundering when seeking swift decisions in war, we have yet to see a smart operation that drags on endlessly.

【注释】

拙：笨。与"巧"相对。《书·周官》："作伪，心劳日拙。"《老子》："大直若屈，大巧若拙，大辩若讷。"巧：虚伪不实。《老子》："绝巧弃利，盗贼无有。"

孙子主张作战要速战速决，力避弄巧成拙，贻误战机，使战争无限期拖延下去。因此，他主张："兵贵胜，不贵久。"

【译文】

用兵作战，不怕笨就怕慢，不能为玩弄智巧而浪费时间。

兵无常势，水无常形

There is no fixed pattern in the use of war tactics, just as there is no constant form in the flow of water.

兵无常势，水无常形。

《孙子·虚实篇》

There is no fixed pattern in the use of war tactics, just as there is no constant form in the flow of water.

【注释】

常势：固定不变的态势。常，恒久，经常。《易·系辞上》："动静有常，刚柔断矣。"

孙子认为用兵的规律像水的流动一样，水流动的规律是避开高处而流向低处，用兵的规律是避开敌人坚实之处而攻击其薄弱的地方。水因地势高低而制约流向，用兵作战则根据敌情而制定取胜方针。

【译文】

用兵作战没有固定不变的态势，就像水的流动没有固定的形状一样。

兵以诈立，以利动
War is a game of deception.

兵以诈立，以利动，以分合为变者也。

《孙子·军争篇》

War is a game of deception. Move when it is advantageous, and disperse and concentrate as necessary to bring about changes in the military situation advantageous to your forces.

【注释】

兵以诈立：用兵打仗当以诡诈多变取胜。立，成立，此处指成功，取胜。

孙子认为用兵作战应以诡诈的方法取得胜利。或分散或集中兵力，随时因势而动。曹操曰："兵无常形，以诡诈为道。"

【译文】

用兵打仗要奇诈多变才能胜利，要根据是否有利决定自己的行动，分散或集中兵力，要随情况而变。

兵者，诡道也

War is a game of deception.

兵者，诡道也。

《孙子·始计篇》

War is a game of deception.

【注释】

诡道：诡诈之道。曹操注曰："兵无常形，以诡诈为道。"

孙子认为用兵作战，是一种诡诈的行动。"能而示之不能，用而示之不用；近而示之远，远而示之近。"均为此道。

【译文】

用兵之道，应以诡诈为行动原则。

兵者，国之大事

War is a question of vital importance to the state...

兵者，国之大事，死生之地，存亡之道，不可不察也。

《孙子·始计篇》

War is a question of vital importance to the state, a matter of life and death, the road to survival or ruin. Hence, it is a subject which calls for careful study.

【注释】

兵：本义指兵械。《说文》："兵，械也。"《老子》："夫兵者，不祥之器。"也指战争。《左传·隐公三年》："有宠而好兵，公弗禁。"也指兵法。《战国策·秦策》："公不论兵，必大困。"注："言不以兵法治士。"本章指战争，也有说指军队。察：考核，调查。《论语·卫灵公》："众恶之，必察焉；众好之，必察焉。"

孙子的战争观包括重战（重视战争、认真探讨研究战争）、慎战（慎重地对待战争）、善战（善于指导战争）三个方面。

【译文】

战争是国家大事，关系到军队和民众的生死，国家的兴衰存亡，不能不认真考察和研究。

兵之情主速

In war, speed is the overriding consideration.

兵之情主速，乘人之不及，由不虞之道，攻其所不戒也。

《孙子·九地篇》

In war, speed is the overriding consideration. This means：Catch the enemy unawares，make your way by unexpected routes and attack him where he is least prepared.

【注释】

情：感情，情绪。《荀子·正名》："性之好、恶、喜、怒、哀、乐谓之情。"引申为事物的本性。《孟子·滕文公上》："夫物之不齐，物之情也。"**由不虞之道**：料想不到的道路。由，经过，通过。不虞，不曾料想，没料到。

【译文】

用兵之理，贵在神速，乘敌人措手不及的时机，走敌人意料不到的道路，攻击敌人没有防备的地方。

兵之所加，如以碫投卵者

By staying clear of the enemy's strong points and striking at his weak points, you will be able to fall upon him like using a whetstone to crush an egg.

兵之所加，如以碫投卵者，虚实是也。

《孙子·兵势篇》

By staying clear of the enemy's strong points and striking at his weak points, you will be able to fall upon him like using a whetstone to crush an egg.

【注释】

以碫投卵：碫（duàn），砺石。以碫投卵，用石头打鸡蛋，比喻以强攻弱必定成功。成语"以碫投卵"出于此。**虚实**：虚和实。《战国策·西周》："夫本末更盛，虚实有时。"这里指强和弱。

【译文】

部队攻击敌人，就像用石头打鸡蛋一样轻而易举，是兵力强弱不同。

不尽知用兵之害者

Those who are not fully aware of the harm in waging war. . .

不尽知用兵之害者，则不能尽知用兵之利也。

《孙子·作战篇》

Those who are not fully aware of the harm in waging war are equally unable to understand fully the method of conducting war advantageously.

【注释】

用兵之害：孙子认为一支十万人的军队在外作战就要千里运送粮食及作战物资，"日费千金"，军队如果不能很快取胜，锐气就会受挫，一旦攻城，就会疲惫不堪。且军队长期在外作战，不仅给国家的财政造成困难，还可能会引起其他诸侯国趁机发兵，造成不可收拾的局面。因此孙子主张善用兵者首先要深知"用兵之害"，才能收到"用兵之利"。

【译文】

不能完全知道用兵害处的人，就不能完全知道用兵的好处。

不可胜者，守也

Invulnerability lies in defense...

不可胜者，守也；可胜者，攻也。守则不足，攻则有余。

《孙子·军形篇》

Invulnerability lies in defense, and opportunity of victory, in attack. One defends when one's strength is inadequate; one attacks when one's strength is abundant.

【注释】

不可胜者：不会被敌人战胜的原因。**守**：防守，守卫。与"攻"相对。《易·坎》："王公设险以守其国。" **守则不足**：采取防守，是由于兵力不足，处于劣势。**攻则有余**：采取进攻，是自己兵力充足，处于优势。

【译文】

不会被敌人战胜的原因，是因为做好了防守的准备。能够战胜敌人，是具备了进攻的条件。采取守势，是由于兵力不足。采取攻势，是兵力充足。

不知军之不可以进而谓之进

He arbitrarily orders his army to advance or retreat
when in fact it should not...

不知军之不可以进而谓之进，不知军之不可以退而谓之退，是谓縻军。

《孙子·谋攻篇》

He arbitrarily orders his army to advance or retreat when in fact it should not, thus hampering the initiative of the army.

【注释】

縻（mí）军：縻绊其军，使军队不能自由行动。注引李筌曰："縻，绊也，不知进退者军必败，如绊骥足，无驰骤也。"

孙子认为国君有三种做法对军队是有害的，"不知军之不可以进而谓之进，不知军之不可以退而谓之退"是其一。

【译文】

（国君）不知道军队不能进攻而命令其进攻，不知道军队不能退却而命令其退却，这叫束缚军队。

不知三军之权而同三军之任

He interferes with the officers' command, unaware of the principle that an army should adopt different···

不知三军之权而同三军之任，则军士疑矣。

《孙子·谋攻篇》

He interferes with the officers' command, unaware of the principle that an army should adopt different tactics according to different circumstances. This will create misgivings in the minds of the officers and men.

【注释】

权：变通，机变。《孟子·离娄上》："嫂溺援之以手者，权也。"同：参与，过问。任：责任，职责。《论语·泰伯》："仁以为己任。"

孙子认为国君有三种做法对军队是有害的，"不知三军之权而同三军之任"是其三。

【译文】

（国君）不懂军事上的权宜机变，而去干预军队的指挥，就会使将士产生疑虑。

不知三軍之事而同三軍之政

He interferes with the administration of the army when he is ignorant of its internal affairs. . .

不知三军之事而同三军之政，则军士惑矣。

《孙子·谋政篇》

He interferes with the administration of the army when he is ignorant of its internal affairs, thus causing confusion among the officers and men.

【注释】

同：参与，过问。惑：疑惑。《论语·颜渊》："既欲其生，又欲其死，是惑也。"

孙子认为国君有三种做法对军队是有害的，"不知三军之事而同三军之政"是其二。

【译文】

（国君）不了解军队内部事物，而去干预军队的行政，就会使将士疑惑不解。

出其所不趨，趨其所不意

Appear at places which the enemy cannot reinforce and where he least expects you.

出其所不趋，趋其所不意。

《孙子·虚实篇》

Appear at places which the enemy cannot reinforce and where he least expects you.

【注释】

出其所不趋：出兵攻击要指向敌人无法救援之处。出，出击。趋，奔赴。这里有仓促之意。有的版本作"出其所必趋"，意谓"出兵攻击敌人一定要迅雷不及掩耳。"趋，急速。《庄子·徐无鬼》："王命相者趋射之。"

孙子认为善于进攻的人，敌人不知道防守什么地方。

【译文】

出兵攻击使敌人无法救援，奔袭出乎敌意料之外。

地形者，兵之助也

Advantageous terrain can be a natural ally in battle.

地形者，兵之助也。料敌致胜，计险隘远近，上将之道也。

《孙子·地形篇》

Advantageous terrain can be a natural ally in battle. Superior military leadership lies in the ability to assess the enemy's situation and create conditions for victory, to analyze natural hazards and calculate distances.

【注释】

助：帮助，辅助。隘：险要之地。上将：高级武官，指军中主将。

【译文】

地形是用兵作战的辅助条件。正确判明敌情，勘察地形险易，计算路程远近，制定取胜计划，这是指挥者的职责。

斗众如斗寡

There is no difference between commanding a large army and a small one.

斗众如斗寡，形名是也。

《孙子·兵势篇》

There is no difference between commanding a large army and a small one. It is a matter of communications, of establishing an efficient system of command signals.

【注释】

形名：旌旗、金鼓。曹操注曰："旌旗曰形，金鼓曰名。"旌旗、金鼓均为军中指挥之具，故形名也作指挥解。《孙子·军争篇》"夫金鼓旌旗者，所以一民之耳目也。"意谓"作战时用语言指挥听不到，所以设置金鼓；用动作指挥看不见，所以设置旌旗。"

【译文】

指挥大兵团作战像指挥小部队作战一样，只是要依靠旌旗、金鼓来代替话语和形体动作指挥而已。

发火有时，起火有日

There is appropriate weather and appropriate days to start a fire.

发火有时，起火有日。时者，天之燥也。日者，月在箕、壁、翼、轸也。

《孙子·火攻篇》

There is appropriate weather and appropriate days to start a fire. Dry weather is best for using fire attacks, and the days when the moon passes through the constellations of the Winnowing Basket, the Wall, the Wings and the Chariot Platform are the best for launching a fire attack because those are generally the days when the winds rise.

【注释】

箕、壁、翼、轸：中国古代星宿名，是二十八宿中的四个。月亮运行到这四个星宿的位置时，就是有风的日子。

【译文】

火攻要看天时，纵火要选好日子。所谓天时指天气干燥。所谓日期，选有风的日子。

凡军必知有五火之变

The army must know which of the five kinds of fire attack to use according to the different situations. . .

凡军必知有五火之变，以数守之。

《孙子·火攻篇》

The army must know which of the five kinds of fire attack to use according to the different situations, and wait for the right time to strike.

【注释】

五火之变：根据五种火攻目标而灵活运用。五火，一曰火人（烧敌人员），二曰火积（烧敌人储备），三曰火辎（烧敌人辎重），四曰火库（烧敌人仓库），五曰火队（烧敌运输设施）。

【译文】

军队必须懂得火攻方法的灵活运用，并根据气象等条件来实施。

凡军好高而恶下

Generally speaking, a maneuvering army prefers high, dry ground to low, wet ground.

凡军好高而恶下，贵阳而贱阴，养生而处实，军无百疾，是谓必胜。

《孙子·行军篇》

Generally speaking, a maneuvering army prefers high, dry ground to low, wet ground; it prizes the sunny side and shuns the shady side, so that food and water will be readily available and remain in ample supply, and men and horses may rest and restore their strength and be free of diseases. These conditions will guarantee victory.

【注释】

好高而恶下：应该占领高地，好使部队处居高临下便于冲击敌人，也便于防守的有利地势。贵阳而贱阴：看重向阳之处，而卑视阴湿地带。贵，重视。阳，向阳干燥的地方。贱，轻视。阴，背阴潮湿的地方。养生而处实：便于为军队补充粮草。

【译文】

大凡部署军队在野外作战，都应该占领居高临下的有利地形，选择向阳干爽之地避开阴冷潮湿之地，靠近水草丰盛便于部队给养补充的地方，全体将士百病不生，这样就能保证获得胜利。

凡先处战地而待敌者佚

Generally speaking，he who first occupies the battlefield and awaits his enemy is rested and prepared...

凡先处战地而待敌者佚，后处战地而趋战者劳。故善战者，致人而不致于人。

《孙子·虚实篇》

Generally speaking, he who first occupies the battlefield and awaits his enemy is rested and prepared; he who comes late to the site and hastens into battle is weary and passive. Therefore, those skilled in war move the enemy rather than allow themselves to be moved by him.

【注释】

战地：作战的地区，战场。**佚：**通"逸"。安乐，安闲。提前进入阵地，就能使自己以逸待劳，掌握战争的主动权。**趋**（cù）：奔，急速。引申为仓促。仓促应战，疲劳被动。**致人而不致于人：**致人，掌握战争的主动权，牵制敌人的弱点，主宰敌人的命运，争取战争的胜利。致于人，表示战争的主动权受制于人，被敌人牵着鼻子走，处于被动挨打的局面。

【译文】

提前进入阵地以佚待劳就主动，后进入阵地仓促应战就被动。所以，善于指挥作战的人，在战场上总是注意因机制敌，先发制人，力争掌握战争的主动权，避免被敌人牵着鼻子走，处于被动挨打的局面。

凡用兵之法，全国为上，破国次之

Generally in war, the best policy is to take the enemy state whole and intact; to destroy it is second-best.

凡用兵之法，全国为上，破国次
之；全军为上，破军次之。

《孙子·谋攻篇》

Generally in war, the best policy is to take the enemy
state whole and intact; to destroy it is second-best. To have
the enemy's army surrender in its entirety is better than to
crush it.

【注释】

全国：保全国家体制。春秋时，主要指都城，或者还包括外城及周围地区。破：
打败，攻克。《墨子·非儒》："齐吴破国之难，伏尸以言术数。"全军：保全军队实
力。次之：差一等。

【译文】

一般指挥战争的原则是：使敌国完整降服为上策，
而击破敌国占领它则差一等；使敌军在保全实力的情况
下降服为上策，而击溃敌军取胜则差一等。

凡战者，以正合，以奇胜

Generally in battle，use normal and regular methods to engage the enemy，and use unusual and unexpected methods to achieve victory.

凡战者，以正合，以奇胜。故善出奇者，无穷如天地，不竭如江海。

《孙子·兵势篇》

Generally in battle, use normal and regular methods to engage the enemy, and use unusual and unexpected methods to achieve victory. The resourcefulness of those skilled in the use of unusual and unexpected methods is as inexhaustible as Heaven and Earth and as unending as the flow of rivers.

【注释】

正合：正，古代用兵，以对阵正面交锋为正。合，古代称交战曰合。《孙子·行军篇》："兵怒而相迎，久而不合，又不相去，必谨察之。"奇：设计邀截袭击。

【译文】

战争，都是以正面相交，以奇兵制胜。善于出奇兵的人，就像天地运行一样变化无穷，像江海一样永不枯竭。

反间者，因其敌间而用之

An internal agent, or double agent, is an enemy spy whom you employ.

反间者，因其敌间而用之。

《孙子·用间篇》

An internal agent, or double agent, is an enemy spy whom you employ.

【注释】

反间：对敌人的间谍使用反间计，达到为我所用。

孙子认为用间有五种方式：有因间，有内间，有反间，有死间，有生间。并说："三军之事，莫亲于间，赏莫厚于间，事莫密于间，非圣贤不能用间，非仁义不能使间，非微妙不能得间之实。"

【译文】

所谓反间，就是诱使敌方间谍为我所用。

方马埋轮，未足恃也

It is unlikely that you can make soldiers fight to the end just by tethering the horses and burying the chariot wheels.

方马埋轮，未足恃也；齐勇若
一，政之道也。

《孙子·九地篇》

It is unlikely that you can make soldiers fight to the end
just by tethering the horses and burying the chariot
wheels. The way of managing an army is to try to make the
strong and the weak achieve a uniform level of courage.

【注释】

方马埋轮：方马，把马缚住；埋轮，埋车。表示固守不退。曹操注曰："方，缚
马也；埋轮，示不动也。"

【译文】

想用缚住马匹把车埋起来以防止士兵溃散的办法是
靠不住的；要使官兵团结如一人，靠的是管理教育。

非利不动，非得不用

Do not go into battle if it is not in the interest of the state.

非利不动，非得不用，非危不战。

《孙子·火攻篇》

Do not go into battle if it is not in the interest of the state. Do not deploy your troops if you are not sure of victory. Do not send them into battle if you are not in danger.

【注释】

非得不用：没有取胜的把握就不轻易用兵。得，取胜。危：危急，凶险。《庄子·则阳》："安危相易，祸福相生。"

孙子认为国君不可因一时恼怒而兴兵，将帅不可因一时愤恨而交战。

【译文】

不是形势对国家有利就不行动，没有胜利的把握不草率用兵，不到危急关头不轻易开战。

非圣智不能用间

He who lacks wisdom cannot use agents. . .

非圣智不能用间，非仁义不能使间，非微妙不能得间之实。

《孙子·用间篇》

He who lacks wisdom cannot use agents；he who is not humane and generous cannot direct agents；he who is not sensitive and alert cannot get the truth out of them.

【注释】

用间（jiàn）：使用间谍。**微妙**：精微深奥。《老子》："古之善为士者，微妙玄通，深不可测。"**得间之实**：得到间谍的真实情报。

【译文】

不是才智超群的人，不能使用间谍。不是仁慈宽厚的人不能利用间谍。不是精于设计、手段巧妙的人无法取得真实情报。

纷纷纭纭，斗乱而不可乱

Amidst the chaos of men and horses locked in battle beneath waving banners, there must be no disorder in command.

纷纷纭纭，斗乱而不可乱；浑浑沌沌，形圆而不可败。

《孙子·兵势篇》

Amidst the chaos of men and horses locked in battle beneath waving banners, there must be no disorder in command. The troops may appear to be milling about in circles, but they should be deployed in a way that guarantees them against defeat.

【注释】

纷纷纭纭：多而纷乱的样子。浑浑沌沌：清浊不分的样子。《庄子·应帝王》："中央之帝为浑沌。"释文："清浊未分也。"

【译文】

战场形势瞬息万变，对付混乱局面首先要自己阵脚不乱；战场情况模糊不清，但布阵得当，就不会失败。

夫兵形像水

Now the law governing military operations is as that governing the flow of water...

孙子说

夫兵形像水，水之形，避高而趋下；兵之形，避实而击虚。水因地而制流，兵因敌而制胜。

《孙子·虚实篇》

Now the law governing military operations is as that governing the flow of water: The flow of water always evades high points, choosing lower ones instead; the art of war is to avoid the enemy's strong points and seek out his weak points. As the water changes its course in accordance with the contours of the terrain, so a strategist changes his tactics in accordance with the enemy's changing situation.

【注释】

兵形像水：用兵的原则像水的流动一样。水流动的规律是避高趋低，用兵作战的规律是避实击虚。

【译文】

用兵的原则像水的流动一样，水流动的规律是避高趋低，而用兵作战的规律是避实击虚。水因地势高低制约其流向，用兵则依据敌情变化而决定作战计划的制定。

夫钝兵挫锐

**When your weapons are blunted and your morale damp-
ened. . .**

夫钝兵挫锐，屈力殚货，则诸侯乘其弊而起，虽有智者不能善其后矣。

《孙子·作战篇》

When your weapons are blunted and your morale damp-ened, neighboring states will take advantage of your distress to strike. In that case, no one, however wise, will be able to a-vert the disastrous consequences which ensue.

【注释】

屈（jué）力殚货：战斗力低下，物资匮乏。殚（dān），尽。《淮南子·说山》："宋君亡其珠，池中鱼为之殚。"货，财货。善其后：指事前考虑周密，后乃可以无患。

【译文】

如果军队疲惫不堪，锐气受挫，战斗力低下，物资匮乏，其他诸侯必定趁机进兵，纵有智者也难以收拾局面。

夫未战而庙算胜者，得算多也

He who makes a full assessment of the situation at the prewar council meeting in the temple is more likely to win.

夫未战而庙算胜者，得算多也；
未战而庙算不胜者，得算少也。

《孙子·始计篇》

He who makes a full assessment of the situation at the prewar council meeting in the temple is more likely to win. He who makes an insufficient assessment of the situation at this meeting is less likely to win.

【注释】

夫（fú）：语气词，置句首，表示要发议论。庙算：由朝廷制定的克敌谋略。"庙算者，计算于庙堂之上也"（唐·杜牧）。庙，朝堂。算，计谋。

【译文】

战前能预料必胜的，是因为帷幄运筹周密，胜利的条件充分；战前就预料不能取胜的，是因为胜利的条件不充分。

夫吳人與越人相惡也

The people of Wu and the people of Yue hate each other.

夫吴人与越人相恶也，当其同舟
而济而遇风，其相救也如左右手。

《孙子·九地篇》

The people of Wu and the people of Yue hate each other. Yet if they were to cross a river in the same boat and were caught in a storm they would come to each other's assistance, as the right hand helps the left.

【注释】

吴人与越人相恶：吴越两国间曾互相攻伐，以致互相亡国，故说两国人"相恶"。**同舟而济**：大家同坐一条船过河。济，渡水。成语"吴越同舟"、"同舟共济"出于此，比喻同心协力共同渡过困难。**左右手**：自己的两只手。后多比喻得力的助手。

【译文】

吴国人和越国人是互相仇恨的，但当他们同船渡河，遇到大风，他们则能互相救援如左右手（因为大家有着同生共死的命运）。

攻其无备，出其不意

Attack when the enemy is least prepared. Take action when he least expects you.

攻其无备，出其不意。此兵家之胜，不可先传也。

《孙子·始计篇》

Attack when the enemy is least prepared. Take action when he least expects you. Herein lies a strategist's subtlety of command, which is impossible to codify in hard-and-fast rules beforehand.

【注释】

攻其无备，出其不意：乘敌无备而进击之。意，料想，猜测。曹操注曰："击其懈怠，出其空虚。"传：传授。

孙子认为作战双方受天时、地利、敌情变化制约，而且这些作战因素又随时随地变化莫测，战争的指挥者要善于掌握敌情动态寻找有利战机适时果断地突然发动攻击，因而他说："不可先传也。"

【译文】

要在敌军意料不到的时机和地方发动突然攻击，这是军事家指挥打仗取胜的奥妙之处，是不能预先传授的。

攻而必取者，攻其所不守也

That you are certain to take what you attack is because you attack a place the enemy cannot protect.

攻而必取者，攻其所不守也；守
而必固者，守其所不攻也。

《孙子·虚实篇》

That you are certain to take what you attack is because
you attack a place the enemy cannot protect. That you are
certain of success in holding what you defend is because you
defend a place the enemy finds impregnable.

【注释】

不守：没有守备。不攻：无法进攻。

孙子认为无论进攻还是防守都要牢牢掌握住战争的主动权，微妙到看不出一丝
形迹，神奇到听不到一点声息。这样进攻，敌人不知如何防守；防守，敌人不知如
何进攻。

【译文】

进攻必定能攻破的，是因为攻击敌人没有防备的地
方。防御必能固守的，是因为扼住了敌人攻击的方向。

挂形者，敌无备，出而胜之

The nature of this terrain gua, which enmeshes, is such that if the enemy is unprepared and you go out to engage him, you might defeat him.

挂形者，敌无备，出而胜之；敌若有备，出而不胜，难以返，不利。

《孙子·地形篇》

The nature of this terrain gua, which enmeshes, is such that if the enemy is unprepared and you go out to engage him, you might defeat him. But when the enemy is prepared and you go out to engage him, you will not only fail to defeat him, but will have difficulty getting out.

【注释】

挂形：孙子把前平后险，便于前进，后退困难的地域称为"挂"。《孙子·地形篇》："可以往，难以返，曰挂。"

【译文】

在挂形地域作战，敌人如无防备，可以突然出击而战胜它；如果敌人有防备，出击而不能取胜，地形又难以退回，就会陷于不利的境地。

国之贫于师者远输

When a country is impoverished by military operations, it is because of the long-distance transportation involved.

国之贫于师者远输，远输而百姓贫。

《孙子·作战篇》

When a country is impoverished by military operations, it is because of the long-distance transportation involved. Transporting supplies over long distances renders the people destitute.

【注释】

远输：远途运送作战物资。

孙子主张远程作战尽量做到"取用于国，因粮于敌"。这样可以避免远程运送粮草的害处。

【译文】

国家因用兵而导致贫困的，远途运送给养是个重要原因，远道运输会使百姓贫困。

厚而不能使，爱而不能令

If a commander indulges his troops to the point at which he cannot use them, if he dotes on them to the point at which he cannot enforce his orders...

厚而不能使，爱而不能令，乱而不能治，譬若骄子，不可用也。

《孙子·地形篇》

If a commander indulges his troops to the point at which he cannot use them, if he dotes on them to the point at which he cannot enforce his orders, if his troops are disorderly and he is unable to control them, they will be as useless as spoiled children.

【注释】

譬若骄子，不可用也：意谓将帅仅对部下施仁爱而不能严加管理，只会使士卒成为"骄子"而不能作战。

【译文】

将帅对士卒过分亲厚而不能使用，一味溺爱而不能令使，违反了纪律也不能严肃处理，这样的军队，就好像"骄子"一样，是不能用来打仗的。

火发上风，无攻下风

If fire is set upwind, do not attack from downwind.

老人家说系列丛书　孙子说

火发上风，无攻下风。

《孙子·火攻篇》

If fire is set upwind, do not attack from downwind.

【注释】

上风：风向的上方，下风：风向的下方。

孙子认为使用火攻，必须掌握风向，否则适得其反。他说："昼风久，夜风止。凡军必知有五火之变，以数守之。"

【译文】

火攻要在风向的上方放火，不能从风向的下方放火。

激水之疾，至于漂石者，势也

Torrential water can move boulders because of its momentum.

激水之疾，至于漂石者，势也；
鸷鸟之疾，至于毁折者，节也。

《孙子·兵势篇》

Torrential water can move boulders because of its momentum. Falcons can strike and kill their prey because of their lightning speed.

【注释】

激水：湍急的流水。激，急疾，猛烈。漂石：浮起漂动石头。漂，浮，浮流。
鸷鸟：猛禽，如鹰、雕之类。节：节奏，节拍。

【译文】

湍急的流水能漂动石头，是水的来势宏大；猛禽能捕杀鸟雀，是其节奏迅猛。

计利以听，乃为之势

Having accepted my assessment of the relative advantages and disadvantages, the general must create a favorable strategic situation which will help bring about victory.

计利以听，乃为之势，以佐其外。势者，因利而制权也。

《孙子·始计篇》

Having accepted my assessment of the relative advantages and disadvantages, the general must create a favorable strategic situation which will help bring about victory. By this I mean being flexible and making the most of advantages to gain the initiative in war.

【注释】

计利以听：筹划周到的谋略被采纳。计，谋略。听，听从，接受。势：态势。佐：辅助，佐助。权：变通，机变。古称道之至当不变者为经，反经合道为权。《公羊传·桓公十一年》："权者何？权者反于经，然后有善者也。"

【译文】

筹划周到的谋略被采纳，但还需要造成一种态势作为外在的辅助条件。所谓有利的态势，就是根据对自己有利的情况，灵活机动地掌握作战的主动权。

间事未发，而先闻者

If plans relating to secret operations are prematurely divulged. . .

间事未发，而先闻者，闻与所告者皆死。

《孙子·用间篇》

If plans relating to secret operations are prematurely divulged, the agent and all those to whom he has leaked the secret should be put to death.

【注释】

间事：派遣间谍的事。闻与所告者：知道派遣间谍事情的人和他告诉这事的人。

孙子认为"事莫密于间"，用间是关系军队、国家生死存亡的大事，不可不严守秘密。

【译文】

派遣间谍的计划还没有执行，就被泄露出去，对泄密者和知情的人都要采取断然措施。

将有五危

There are five weaknesses of character for a commander.

将有五危：必死，可杀也；必生，可虏也；忿速，可侮也；廉洁，可辱也；爱民，可烦也。

《孙子·九变篇》

There are five weaknesses of character for a commander. If he is stubborn and reckless, he may be deceived and killed. If he fears death more than anything else, he may be captured. If he is hot-tempered, he may be provoked. If he is honest but has too delicate a sense of honor, he is open to insult. If he is too compassionate toward his people, he may be easily troubled and upset.

【注释】

必死：只知死拼，有勇无谋。**必生**：贪生怕死，临阵畏缩。**忿速**：忿怒急躁。

【译文】

将帅有五种致命的弱点：有勇无谋，只知拼命，就可能被敌人诱杀；临阵畏怯，贪生怕死，就可能被敌俘虏；急躁易怒，一触即跳，就可能被敌人凌侮而妄动；廉洁好名，过于自尊，就可能被敌人污辱而失去理智；只知"爱民"，就可能被敌人烦忧而陷于被动。

校之以计，而索其情

When assessing the outcome of a war compare the two sides. . .

校之以计，而索其情，曰：主孰有道？将孰有能？天地孰得？法令孰行？兵众孰强？士卒孰练？赏罚孰明？

《孙子·始计篇》

When assessing the outcome of a war, compare the two sides in terms of the following seven factors, and appraise the situation accordingly: Find out which sovereign possesses more moral influence, which general is more capable, which side has the advantage of Heaven and Earth, which army is better disciplined, whose troops are better armed and trained, and which command is more impartial in meting out rewards and punishments.

【注释】

主：君主。古时称诸侯为社稷主，天子为天下主。能：才能。得：合适，有利。行（xíng）：实行，执行。兵：兵器。强：胜过，优良。练：使熟练。

【译文】

通过对敌我双方七种情况的比较，来探索战争的胜负因素。这七种情况是：看哪一方君主更清明？哪一方的将帅更有能力？天时地利对哪一方更有利？哪一方贯彻法令更坚决？哪一方武器更精良？哪一方士卒更加训练有素？哪一方赏罚更加严明？

进而不可御者，冲其虚也

His advance is irresistible because he plunges into his enemy's weak position.

进而不可御者，冲其虚也；退而不可追者，速而不可及也。

《孙子·虚实篇》

His advance is irresistible because he plunges into his enemy's weak position; and he cannot be overtaken during withdrawal because it is so swift.

【注释】

冲其虚也：攻击敌人力量薄弱的地方。

【译文】

进攻而敌人无法抵抗的，是因为攻击点选在了敌人力量薄弱的地方；撤退而敌人无法追赶的，是因为我军行动迅速敌人追赶不上。

经之以五事

To assess the outcome of a war，examine and compare the two sides in terms of the following five factors.

经之以五事，校之以计，而索其情：一曰道，二曰天，三曰地，四曰将，五曰法。

《孙子·始计篇》

To assess the outcome of a war, examine and compare the two sides in terms of the following five factors: The first is the Tao; the second, Heaven; the third, Earth; the fourth, command; and the fifth, rules and regulations.

【注释】

经：经历，经过。校（jiào）：计较，比较。索：探索，研究。道：政治。天：天时。地：地利。将：将领。指将帅的智谋、诚信、仁慈、勇敢、严明。法：法制。指军队的组织编制、管理以及军需的供应等。

【译文】

要经过敌我五个方面因素的分析，进行比较而确定计谋，研究战争胜负的情势。这五个方面包括：政治，天时，地利，将领，法制。

九地之变

The different handling of the nine kinds of regions. . .

九地之变，屈伸之利，人情之理，不可不察。

《孙子·九地篇》

The different handling of the nine kinds of regions, the advantages and disadvantages of being on the offensive or on the defensive and the vagaries of human nature—they must all be thoroughly looked into.

【注释】

　　九地：孙子将战地分为散地、轻地、争地、交地、衢地、重地、圮地、围地、死地等九类。

【译文】

　　根据不同地形地势采取不同的行动方针，适应情况，伸缩进退，择其所利，掌握士卒在不同的情况下的人情常理。这些都不能不认真审察和仔细研究。

绝地无留

The army should not linger in enemy-occupied areas. . .

孙子说

绝地无留，围地则谋，死地则战。

《孙子·九变篇》

The army should not linger in enemy-occupied areas; you should have contingency plans when passing through the areas where the enemy is able to defeat a strong army with fewer troops; you should fight desperately with the enemy where there is no other way out.

【注释】

绝地：极为险恶而无出路的境地。《孙子·九地篇》："去国越境而师者，绝地也。"围地：山川环绕，四周险峻之地。死地：必死之地。《孙子·九地篇》："投之亡地然后存，陷之死地然后生。"

【译文】

行军在险恶而无出路的地方不要停留，要赶快通过；在山川环绕，四周险峻容易被包围的地方要运用谋略；陷入必死之地则要坚决作战，陷之死地而后生。

军无辎重则亡

An army without its equipment，food and fodder，and material reserves cannot survive.

军无辎重则亡，无粮食则亡，无委积则亡。

《孙子·军争篇》

An army without its equipment, food and fodder, and material reserves cannot survive.

【注释】

辎重：行军携带的物资，常指军用物资。**委积：**物资储备。

【译文】

行军打仗没有军用物资就要失败，没有粮食就要失败，没有军需物资储备就要失败。

客绝水而来

When the advancing enemy is crossing a river. . .

客绝水而来，勿迎之于水内，令半济而击之，利。

《孙子·行军篇》

When the advancing enemy is crossing a river, do not meet him in the river; it is to your advantage to wait until he is half-way across, and then strike.

【注释】

客：此处指敌军。半济：渡河渡过一半。济，渡过。《左传·文公三年》："秦伯伐晋，济河焚舟。"

【译文】

如果敌军渡河向我进攻，我军就不应在河面上截击，而要等敌军半数渡河后，趁其立足未稳，发起攻击，此时攻击对我军最为有利。

其疾如风，其徐如林

When the army advances, it is as swift as the wind;
when it is immobile, as still as the forest.

其疾如风，其徐如林，侵掠如火，不动如山，难知如阴，动如雷震。

《孙子·军争篇》

When the army advances, it is as swift as the wind; when it is immobile, as still as the forest; when it attacks, as destructive as a fire; when it defends, as immovable as a mountain; when it conceals itself, it is as though hidden behind an overcast sky; and when it strikes, it can be as sudden as a thunderbolt.

【注释】

徐：缓慢。《左传·昭公二十年》："清浊大小，短长疾徐……以相济也。"侵掠：以强力夺取。

【译文】

军队行动快如疾风，慢如山林严整从容，进攻如迅猛的烈火，守如山岳屹立不动，隐藏如黑夜不见日月星辰，冲锋如万钧雷霆。

其用战也，胜久则钝兵挫锐

In a war involving a huge army, the main objective should be quick victory.

其用战也，胜久则钝兵挫锐，攻城则力屈，久暴师则国用不足。

《孙子·作战篇》

In a war involving a huge army, the main objective should be quick victory. If the war is prolonged, the weapons will be blunted and the men's morale will be dampened. When they attack cities, their strength will be exhausted. Protracted campaigns will be a serious strain on the treasury.

【注释】

钝兵挫锐：钝兵，谓兵刃钝弊。《战国策·楚策二》："弊甲钝兵，愿承下尘。"挫，受挫折。《管子·五辅》："是以小者兵挫而地削，大者身死而国亡。"**力屈**（jué）：力量耗尽。屈，竭尽，穷尽。**暴**（pù）**师**：指军队在外，蒙受风霜雨露。

【译文】

开战后，如果不能速胜，部队的锐气就会受到挫折。一旦攻城，则力量将会消耗尽。军队长久在外，国家就会财政困难。

三军可夺气，将军可夺心

An entire army can be demoralized and its general deprived of his presence of mind.

老人家说系列丛书 孙子说

三军可夺气，将军可夺心。是故朝气锐，昼气惰，暮气归。

《孙子·军争篇》

An entire army can be demoralized and its general deprived of his presence of mind. At the beginning of a campaign, the soldiers' morale is high, after a while it begins to flag, and in the end it is gone.

【注释】

夺气：慑于声威，丧失胆气。夺心：丧失信心。朝气锐，昼气惰，暮气归：朝，初。昼，白天，中午。暮，旁晚。

【译文】

三军可以挫伤其锐气，将军可以动摇其决心。军队初战时士气旺盛，过一阵子就逐渐懈怠，到了后期，士卒就会气竭思归。

三军之事，莫亲于间

Of all those in the army close to the commander, nobody is more intimate than the agent.

三军之事，莫亲于间，赏莫厚于间，事莫密于间。

《孙子·用间篇》

Of all those in the army close to the commander, nobody is more intimate than the agent; of all rewards, none are more liberal than those given to the agent; of all matters, none are more confidential than those relating to secret operations.

【注释】

亲：近，亲近。《论语·学而》："泛爱众而亲仁。" 厚：优厚，多。 密：慎密，机密。《易·系辞上》："凡事不密则害成。"

【译文】

军中最亲近的人无过于委派为间谍的，赏赐没有比间谍更优厚的，没有比使用间谍更机密的事。

三军之众，可使必受敌而无败者

the army is able to withstand the onslaught of the enemy
forces.

三军之众，可使必受敌而无败者，奇正是也。

《孙子·兵势篇》

Thanks to the combined use of unusual and unexpected tactics and normal and regular methods, the army is able to withstand the onslaught of the enemy forces.

【注释】

奇（qí）正：古代用兵，以对阵交锋为正，使计奇袭为奇。《孙子·兵势篇》："战势不过奇正，奇正之变，不可胜穷也。"

【译文】

指挥作战不会失败，靠的是对阵正面交锋和设计邀截奇袭相结合的战术。

善攻者，敌不知其所守

Against the expert in attack, the enemy does not know where to defend...

善攻者，敌不知其所守；善守者，敌不知其所攻。

《孙子·虚实篇》

Against the expert in attack, the enemy does not know where to defend; and against the expert in defense, the enemy does not know where to attack.

【注释】

孙子认为无论进攻还是防守都要牢牢掌握住战争的主动权，微妙到看不出一丝形迹，神奇到听不出一点声息。这样进攻，敌人不知如何防守；防守，敌人不知如何进攻。

【译文】

善于进攻的，使敌人不知道如何防守；善于防守的，使敌人不知道如何进攻。

善守者，藏于九地之下

He who is skilled in defense positions his forces in places as safe and inaccessible as in the depths of the Earth...

善守者，藏于九地之下；善攻者，动于九天之上，故能自保而全胜也。

《孙子·军形篇》

He who is skilled in defense positions his forces in places as safe and inaccessible as in the depths of the Earth, whereas he who is skilled in attack strikes as from the highest reaches of Heaven. In this way, he is able both to protect himself and to win complete victory.

【注释】

藏（cáng）：潜匿，隐藏。九地：九地在《孙子》中有两个意思，一指用兵之九种地势，见《九地篇》；一种指地下最深处，极言其深，不会被发现。动：行动。九天：极言其高。

【译文】

善于防守的人，深沟高垒好像把兵力藏在深深的地下一样。善于进攻的人，迅速猛烈好像兵力从天上突然降临敌阵一样。居高临下，势如破竹，所以他既能保存自己，又能取得全胜。

善用兵者，譬如率然

Those who are skilled in employing troops are like the snake found on Mount Chang.

善用兵者，譬如率然。率然者，常山之蛇也。击其首则尾至，击其尾则首至，击其中则首尾俱至。

《孙子·九地篇》

Those who are skilled in employing troops are like the snake found on Mount Chang. If you strike at its head, its tail will come to help; it you strike at its tail, its head will come to help; and if you strike at its middle, both head and tail will come to the rescue.

【注释】

率然：蛇名。喻一种阵法，称作"常山蛇阵"。《晋书·桓温传》："初，诸葛亮造八阵图于鱼复平沙之上，垒石为八行，行相去二丈。温见之，谓'此常山蛇势也'。"

【译文】

善于用兵打仗的人，布阵就像"率然"一样。所谓"率然"，就是常山蛇，打它的头尾巴来接应，打它的尾巴头就来接应，打它的中间，首尾都来接应。

善用兵者，屈人之兵而非战也

He who is skilled in war subdues the enemy without fighting.

善用兵者，屈人之兵而非战也，拔人之城而非攻也，毁人之国而非久也，必以全争于天下，故兵不顿而利可全，此谋攻之法也。

《孙子·谋攻篇》

He who is skilled in war subdues the enemy without fighting. He captures the enemy's cities without assaulting them. He overthrows the enemy's kingdom without prolonged operations in the field. By taking all under Heaven with his "whole and intact strategy," he wins total victory without wearing out his troops. This is the method of attacking by stratagem.

【注释】

故兵不顿而利可全：顿，通"钝"。《墨子·辞过》："兵革不顿，士兵不劳，是以征不服。"引申为军队疲惫受挫。利，利益。全，促使，万全。

【译文】

善于用兵的人，能够不战而使敌人屈服，不靠强攻而能占领敌人的城池，不经长久攻伐而能灭亡敌国，保证占有一个完整的天下。使自己不致疲惫受挫而能取得全胜，这才是谋攻的最高原则。

善用兵者，修道而保法

He who is skilled in deploying troops seeks victory by cultivating the Tao and strengthening rules and regulations. . .

善用兵者，修道而保法，故能为
胜败之敌。

《孙子·军形篇》

He who is skilled in deploying troops seeks victory by
cultivating the Tao and strengthening rules and regulations,
and in so doing, gains the initiative over his enemy.

【注释】

修道：修，学习，遵循。《礼·学记》："君子之于学也，藏焉，修焉。"注：
"修，习也。"道，规律，事理。

【译文】

善于用兵的人，能够加强内部团结，保障各种制度
的贯彻执行，所以他能主宰胜败。

善用兵者，役不再籍

Those adept at waging war do not require a second conscription or replenishment of provisions from the home country.

善用兵者，役不再籍，粮不三载，取用于国，因粮于敌，故军食可足也。

《孙子·作战篇》

Those adept at waging war do not require a second conscription or replenishment of provisions from the home country. They obtain their military supplies from home, but commandeer provisions from the enemy territory. Thus, their army will always be plentifully supplied.

【注释】

役不再籍：不用再次从国内征兵。役，服兵役。再，二次，又。籍，登记，征集。粮不三载：不多次从国内运送粮食。载，装载。取用于国，因粮于敌：从敌人那里取得作战物资和粮食以补充军队。

孙子认为"智将务食于敌"。

【译文】

善于用兵的人，不用第二次征兵，不用多次从国内运送粮食，要从敌人那里取得作战物资和粮食补充自己，使军队粮饷充足。

善战人之势，如转圆石于千仞之山者

He who is skilful in turning the situation to his advantage can send his men into battle as he would roll logs or rocks. . .

善战人之势，如转圆石于千仞之山者，势也。

《孙子·兵势篇》

He who is skilful in turning the situation to his advantage can send his men into battle as he would roll logs or rocks down from mountain heights.

【注释】

转圆石：转动圆形石头。喻便易迅速。"木石之性，安则静，危则动，方则止，圆则行。"（《孙子·兵势篇》）意谓：木石的性情是处于平坦之地就静止，处于陡峭倾斜之地就滚动，方形容易停止，圆形容易滚动。故说从"千仞之山"上滚动圆石，以喻其势。

【译文】

会带兵打仗的人创造态势，就像在高山上设置檑木炮石，居高临下，势不可挡。

善战者，立于不败之地

He who is skilled in deploying troops puts himself in a position in which he cannot be defeated...

善战者，立于不败之地，而不失敌之败也。

《孙子·军形篇》

He who is skilled in deploying troops puts himself in a position in which he cannot be defeated, and misses no opportunity to defeat his enemy.

【注释】

不失敌之败也：不放过任何一个打败敌人的机会。

孙子认为善战者取胜是必然的，因为他所战胜的是已经陷于必败境地的敌人。

【译文】

善于指挥打仗的人，总是先使自己立于不败之地，而不放过任何一个打败敌人的机会。

善战者，其势险，其节短

When launching an offensive, a good commander creates a good posture which provides him with an irresistible momentum, and when he attacks, it is with lighting speed.

善战者，其势险，其节短。势如
彍弩，节如发机。

《孙子·兵势篇》

When launching an offensive, a good commander creates a good posture which provides him with an irresistible momentum, and when he attacks, it is with lighting speed. The momentum is like that of a fully drawn crossbow, and the speed like that of the arrow leaving the bow.

【注释】

其势险：使部队造成居高临下的险峻态势。**其节短：**其冲击节奏急骤。**彍弩：**彍（guō），拉满弓。弩，用机械力量发射箭的弓，力强可以及远。**发机：**机，即弩牙。拨动弩牙，将弩箭突然射出。

【译文】

善于指挥作战的人，总是把军队布置成有利的阵势，便于急速出击。像拉开弓弩那样蓄势，像拨动弩牙那样突然发射。

善战者，求之于势

One who is skilled at directing war always tries to turn the situation to his advantage...

善战者，求之于势，不责于人，故能择人而任势。

《孙子·兵势篇》

One who is skilled at directing war always tries to turn the situation to his advantage rather than make excessive demands on his subordinates. Hence, he is able to select the right men and exploit the situation.

【注释】

求之于势，不责于人：势，态势。把注意力放在如何利用地势上，把部队部署在居高临下的态势，而不是苛责士卒。

【译文】

善于指挥作战的人，他依靠态势，而不苛求于个人，能选用适当的人才创造好的态势。

上兵伐谋

The best policy in war is to thwart the enemy's strategy.

上兵伐谋，其次伐交，其次伐兵，其下攻城。

《孙子·谋攻篇》

The best policy in war is to thwart the enemy's strategy. The second-best policy is to disrupt his alliances through diplomatic means. The third-best policy is to attack his army in the field. The worst policy of all is to attack a walled city.

【注释】

上兵：用兵的上策。张预曰："言以奇策秘笈，取胜于不战，兵之上也。"**次**：顺序叙事，后项对前项移次。**伐谋**：破坏敌人的计划。**伐交**：破坏敌人和它盟国的邦交。**伐兵**：和敌人交战。**下**：劣等，下策。

【译文】

用兵的上策是破坏敌人的谋略，其次是破坏敌人和它盟国的邦交，再次就是直接和敌兵交战取胜，下策是攻打敌人的城池。

胜兵先胜而后求战

A victorious army will not engage the enemy unless it is assured of the necessary conditions for victory...

胜兵先胜而后求战，败兵先战而后求胜。

《孙子·军形篇》

A victorious army will not engage the enemy unless it is assured of the necessary conditions for victory, whereas an army destined for defeat rushes into battle in the hope that it will win by luck.

【注释】

胜兵先胜而后求战：胜兵，打胜仗的军队。先胜而后求战，先创造取胜的条件然后再和敌人作战。

【译文】

打胜仗的军队，总是先创造条件使自己立于不败之地，而后才同敌人作战；打败仗的军队，总是仓促作战，而后求侥幸取胜。

胜者之战，若决积水于千仞之溪

A victorious army goes into battle with the force of an onrushing torrent，which，when suddenly released，plunges into a chasm a thousand fathoms deep.

胜者之战，若决积水于千仞之溪者，形也。

《孙子·军形篇》

A victorious army goes into battle with the force of an onrushing torrent, which, when suddenly released, plunges into a chasm a thousand fathoms deep. This is what we mean by disposition.

【注释】

仞（rèn）：长度单位。《书·旅獒》："为山九仞，功亏一篑。"仞的长度说法不一，有说七尺为一仞，有说八尺为一仞。形：形势，地势。《战国策·西周》："周君形不小利事秦，而好小利。"宋·鲍彪注："形，势也。"

【译文】

胜利者在指挥打仗的时候，就像从几千尺的高处决开溪中积水一样，其势猛不可挡。这是强大的军事实力的表现。

始如处女，敌人开户

Before action starts, appear as shy as a maiden, and the enemy will relax his vigilance and leave his door open.

始如处女，敌人开户；后如脱兔，敌不及拒。

《孙子·九地篇》

Before action starts, appear as shy as a maiden, and the enemy will relax his vigilance and leave his door open; once the fighting begins, move as swiftly as a scurrying rabbit, and the enemy will find it too late to put up a resistance.

【注释】

始如处女：开始如处女般柔弱沉静以麻痹敌人，使敌人放松戒备。后如脱兔：然后像逃脱的兔子一样迅速狂奔，使敌人来不及抗拒。

【译文】

对敌作战开始前像深闺的处女一样沉静以示其弱，使敌人麻痹大意而放松戒备，暴露出可攻击的弱点。然后要像逃脱的兔子一样狂奔出击，使敌人来不及抗拒。

视卒如婴儿

Because the commander cares for his soldiers as if they were his children, they will follow him through the greatest dangers.

视卒如婴儿，故可以与之赴深溪；视卒如爱子，故可与之俱死。

《孙子·地形篇》

Because the commander cares for his soldiers as if they were his children, they will follow him through the greatest dangers. Because he loves his soldiers as if they were his own sons, they will stand by him even unto death.

【注释】

卒：士卒，兵士。婴儿：小孩子。深溪：水深。溪，山间河沟。喻危险地带。爱子：心爱的儿子。

【译文】

将帅对待士卒能够像对待小孩儿那样爱护，士卒就可以跟随将帅赴汤蹈火；将帅对待士卒能够像对待自己心爱的儿子一样，士卒就可以与将帅同生死，共患难。

通形者，先居高阳

On a terrain of tong which is accessible，he who first occupies the sunny，high ground and establishes convenient
supply routes has the advantage in battle.

通形者，先居高阳，利粮道，以战则利。

《孙子·地形篇》

On a terrain of tong which is accessible, he who first occupies the sunny, high ground and establishes convenient supply routes has the advantage in battle.

【注释】

通形：孙子把地形分为通、挂、支、隘、险、远六种。敌我双方都可以通达的地域叫做"通形"。**高阳**：地势高而向阳之地。**利粮道**：便利运送粮草的通道。

【译文】

在通形地域作战，要抢先占领地势高而向阳的有利地势，沟通并保护好运送粮草的通道，这样与敌交战就有利。

投之亡地然后存

Only when you throw the troops into a life-and-death situation will they fight to survive.

投之亡地然后存，陷之死地然后生。

《孙子·九地篇》

Only when you throw the troops into a life-and-death situation will they fight to survive. Only when you plunge them into places where there is no way out will they fight to stay alive.

【注释】

亡地：危地，绝境。**陷之死地然后生**：地势险恶，只有奋勇作战才能生存，不迅速力战就难免覆灭的地区，叫"死地"。

【译文】

把军队投入危亡境地，然后人自为战而得存；把士卒陷入死绝之地，然后人皆奋勇作战而得生还。

途有所不由，军有所不击

There are roads the commander should not take，armies he should not attack...

途有所不由，军有所不击，城有所不攻，地有所不争，君命有所不受。

《孙子·九变篇》

There are roads the commander should not take, armies he should not attack, walled cities he should not assault, territories he should not contest for, and commands of the king he should not obey.

【注释】

途有所不由：有的道路不可以通过。途，道路。《孙子·军争篇》："故迂其途而诱之以利。"由，自，从。《论语·雍也》："谁能出不由户者，何莫由斯道也。"

【译文】

指挥部队作战相机行事，有的路不能走，有的敌人不可攻击，有的城池不便于攻打，有些地方不一定要争夺，有时国君的命令也可以不服从。

为客之道

The general rule of operation for an invading force is that. . .

为客之道，深则专，浅则散。

《孙子·九地篇》

The general rule of operation for an invading force is that the deeper your penetration into enemy territory, the greater the cohesion of your troops; the shallower the penetration, the slacker and more dispersive your forces.

【注释】

为客之道：进入敌国作战的原则。深则专，浅则散：深入敌国越远，士兵越能专心一志；进入敌国境内越浅，士兵越容易心志散漫。

【译文】

进入敌国作战的原则：进入敌境越深，士兵越能专心一志；进入敌国越浅，士兵越容易心志散漫。

惟明君贤将，能以上智为间者

Only the enlightened king and wise commander who are capable of using the most intelligent people as agents are destined to accomplish great things.

惟明君贤将，能以上智为间者，必成大功。

《孙子·用间篇》

Only the enlightened king and wise commander who are capable of using the most intelligent people as agents are destined to accomplish great things.

【注释】

上智：具有大智慧的人。《韩非子·五蠹》："微妙之言，上智所难知也。"

孙子认为商朝的兴起，是由于伊尹曾在夏朝很久；周朝的兴起，是由于姜尚曾在殷朝很久。后来伊尹佐商汤伐夏桀，姜尚佐周武王伐殷纣王都起到了"用间"的作用。

【译文】

惟有英明的国君、贤能的将帅，能用大智的人作间谍，因而一定能成就大的功业。

我欲战，敌虽高垒深沟

When we want to start battle, the enemy cannot but leave his position to engage us even though he is safe behind high walls and deep moats...

我欲战，敌虽高垒深沟，不得不与我战者，攻其所必救也；我不欲战，虽画地而守之，敌不得与我战者，乘其所之也。

《孙子·虚实篇》

When we want to start battle, the enemy cannot but leave his position to engage us even though he is safe behind high walls and deep moats, because we attack a position he must rescue. When we want to avoid battle, we may simply draw a line on the ground by way of defence, and the enemy cannot engage us because we have diverted him to a different target.

【注释】

画地而守之：据地而守。画，界限，指画出界限。乘其所之也：调动敌人，将其引往他处。乘，违，相反，此处有改变、调动的意思。之，往，去。

【译文】

我军要战，敌人即使高垒深沟坚守，也不得不脱离阵地与我交战，因为我所攻击的是敌人必须要救援的地方；我军若不想交战，即使划地防守，敌人也无法与我交战，因为我已设法诱使敌人改变了进攻的方向。

无所不备，则无所不寡

An army which has to prepare against the enemy everywhere is bound to be weak everywhere.

无所不备，则无所不寡。

《孙子·虚实篇》

An army which has to prepare against the enemy everywhere is bound to be weak everywhere.

【注释】

寡：少。

孙子认为指挥作战应该虚张声势让敌人处处设防，处处设防，就处处兵力少了，这样就为选定攻击目标提供了有利条件。

【译文】

处处防备，就处处兵力薄弱，等于处处无所防备。

无邀正正之旗

Do not intercept an enemy whose banners are in perfect array.

无邀正正之旗，勿击堂堂之陈，此治变者也。

《孙子·军争篇》

Do not intercept an enemy whose banners are in perfect array, and refrain from attacking a powerful army in full formation. This is the way to cope with the question of flexibility.

【注释】

邀：阻截。正正之旗：指旗帜齐整、部署周密的敌人。堂堂之陈：指阵容严整、实力雄厚的敌人。陈，阵。

【译文】

不去拦阻旗帜整齐、部署周密的敌人，不去攻击阵容严整、实力雄厚的敌人，这是掌握机动变化的方法。

先知者，不可取于鬼神

Foreknowledge cannot be obtained from ghosts or spirits. . .

先知者，不可取于鬼神，不可象于事，不可验于度，必取于人，知敌之情者也。

《孙子·用间篇》

Foreknowledge cannot be obtained from ghosts or spirits, nor from gods, nor by analogy with past events, nor from astrological calculations. It can only come from men who know the enemy's situation.

【注释】

先知：预先知道敌情。不可验于度：不能用验证日月星辰运行位置的办法去求知敌情。验，应验，验证。度，度数，指日月星辰的位置。

【译文】

要事先掌握敌情，不能向鬼神卜问，也不能用其它事情作类比去揣测敌情，更不能靠观测星象来判定。必须从那些了解敌情的人中获取情报。

小敌之坚，大敌之擒也

No matter how stubbornly a small force may fight, it must in the end succumb to greater strength, and fall captive to it.

小敌之坚，大敌之擒也。

《孙子·谋攻篇》

No matter how stubbornly a small force may fight, it must in the end succumb to greater strength, and fall captive to it.

【注释】

小敌之坚：弱小军队的坚守。

孙子认为当自己的兵力少于敌人时就要主动退却，兵力弱于敌人时就要避免作战。

【译文】

弱小的军队在强敌面前只知坚守硬拼，势必为强敌所虏。

行火必有因

To launch a fire attack，certain conditions are required.

行火必有因，烟火必素具。

《孙子·火攻篇》

To launch a fire attack, certain conditions are required. Materials for setting the fire must always be on hand.

【注释】

行火：实施以火攻敌。《孙子·火攻篇》："凡火攻有五：一曰火人，二曰火积，三曰火辎，四曰火库，五曰火队。"烟火必素具：火攻用的器材必须经常准备好。烟火，指火攻所必备的燃料器材等物。素，平素，经常。具，准备好。

【译文】

实施火攻必须具备一定的条件，用于火攻的器材必须经常准备好。

形人而我无形

If we are able to determine the enemy's disposition while concealing our own. . .

形人而我无形，则我专而敌分。我专为一，敌分为十，是以十攻其一也。

《孙子·虚实篇》

If we are able to determine the enemy's disposition while concealing our own, then we can concentrate our forces while his are dispersed. And if our forces are concentrated in one place while his are scattered in ten places, then it is ten to one when we attack him in one place. This means that we will be numerically superior.

【注释】

形人而我无形：让敌人暴露目标而我军不露痕迹。形，显露。《荀子·劝学》："故声无小而不闻，行无隐而不形。"专：专一。

【译文】

让敌人暴露目标而我军不露痕迹，这样我军兵力就可以集中而敌人兵力就不得不分散；我军兵力集中在一起，敌军兵力分散十处，这样我就可以用十倍于敌的兵力去攻击敌人，造成我众敌寡的有利态势。

以火佐攻者明

Using fire to assist in attacks can produce notable results. . .

以火佐攻者明，以水佐攻者强。水可以绝，不可以夺。

《孙子·火攻篇》

Using fire to assist in attacks can produce notable results; using the method of inundation can make the attacks more powerful. However, while inundation can cut an enemy off, it cannot deprive him of his supplies and equipment.

【注释】

明：明显，显著。《战国策·齐策》："则秦不能害齐，亦已明矣。" 强：强大，强盛。《孟子·梁惠王上》："晋国天下莫强焉。" 绝：断绝，隔断。

【译文】

用火辅助进攻，效果显著；用水辅助进攻，威力强大。但水只能断绝敌人的联系，却不能夺取敌人的蓄积。

以近待远，以佚待劳

Being close to the battlefield, he awaits an enemy coming from afar...

以近待远，以佚待劳，以饱待饥，此治力者也。

《孙子·军争篇》

Being close to the battlefield, he awaits an enemy coming from afar; well rested, he awaits an exhausted enemy; with well-fed troops, he awaits hungry ones. This is how he copes with the question of strength.

【注释】

以佚待劳：指作战时养精蓄锐，待敌人疲惫后，相机出击。成语也作"以逸待劳"。

【译文】

以自己从容休整等待长途跋涉的敌人，以自己的养精蓄锐等待敌人疲惫，以自己粮食充足等待敌人粮尽人饥，这是掌握军队战斗力的方法。

以治待乱，以静待哗

In good order, he awaits a disorderly enemy...

以治待乱，以静待哗，此治心
者也。

《孙子·军争篇》

In good order, he awaits a disorderly enemy; with calm-
ness, he awaits a clamorous enemy. This is how he copes with
the question of morale.

【注释】

以静待哗：哗，喧哗，哗变。指作战时严整自己的军队，待敌人浮躁哗变后，
相机出击。

【译文】

以自己的严整来对待敌人的混乱，以自己的镇静来
对待敌人的轻躁，这是掌握军心的方法。

用兵之法，十则围之

The art of using troops is: when you outnumber the enemy ten to one, surround him.

用兵之法，十则围之，五则攻之，倍则分之，敌则能战之，少则能逃之，不若则能避之。

《孙子·谋攻篇》

The art of using troops is: when you outnumber the enemy ten to one, surround him; when five to one, attack him; when two to one, divide him; if equally matched, stand up to him; and if fewer than the enemy in number, withdraw.

【注释】

十则围之：兵力十倍于敌就包围敌人。之，代指敌人。

【译文】

用兵的原则是：兵力十倍于敌就包围敌人而歼灭之；兵力五倍于敌就可以大胆进攻敌人；拥有两倍于敌的兵力就设法对敌人分而歼之；兵力和敌人相等应慎重应敌；兵力少于敌人要主动退却；兵力弱于敌人要避免作战。

用兵之法，无恃其不来

It is a rule in war that you must not count on the enemy not coming. . .

　　用兵之法，无恃其不来，恃吾有以待之；无恃其不攻，恃吾有所不可攻也。

《孙子·九变篇》

　　It is a rule in war that you must not count on the enemy not coming, but always be ready for him; that you must not count on the enemy not attacking, but make yourself so strong that you are invincible.

【注释】

　　恃：依赖。《庄子·列御寇》："河上有家贫恃纬萧而食者。"

【译文】

　　用兵的原则是：不抱敌人不会来的侥幸心理，而依靠自己有充分的准备，不怕敌人来；不抱敌人不会攻击的侥幸心理，而依靠自己稳固的防御，能够不被攻破。

用间有五

There are five kinds of spies...

用间有五：有因间、有内间、有反间、有死间、有生间。五间俱起，莫知其道，是谓神纪，人君之宝也。

《孙子·用间篇》

There are five kinds of spies, namely, the native, the internal, the converted, the expendable and the surviving agents. When these five kinds of agents operate simultaneously and in total secrecy in their methods of operation, they can work miracles. This magic weapon is a real treasure for a king.

【注释】

因间：间谍的一种，即"乡间"。指依赖与敌人的乡亲关系获取情报，或利用敌军将领的同乡做间谍。内间：收买敌方官吏做间谍。反间：利用敌方间谍为我所用。死间：故意散布假情报，通过我方间谍把假情报传给敌人，诱使敌人上当，一旦真情败露，我方间谍难免一死，故称死间。生间：侦察敌情后能活着回来的谍报人员。

【译文】

使用间谍有五种情况：有因间、有内间、有反间、有死间、有生间。五种间谍同时使用起来，使敌人无法捉摸我军的行动规律，神妙莫测，这种神妙的方法是国君克敌制胜的法宝。

战道必胜

If the way of war guarantees you victory...

战道必胜，主曰无战，必战可也；战道不胜，主曰必战，无战可也。故进不求名，退不避罪，唯民是保，而利于主，国之宝也。

《孙子·地形篇》

If the way of war guarantees you victory, it is right for you to insist on fighting even if the king has forbidden it. Where the way of war does not allow for victory, it is right for you to refuse to fight even if the king says you must. Therefore, a commander who decides to advance without any thought of winning personal fame and to withdraw without fear of punishment, and whose only concern is to protect his people and serve his king is an invaluable asset to the state.

【注释】

战道必胜：根据战场实情确有必胜的把握。

【译文】

如果根据战场实际情况确有必胜的把握，即使国君命令不许打，也要坚决打；如果根据战场实际情况不能取胜，即使国君命令打，也坚决不打。所以，作为主帅，进不求名誉，退不避责任，只求保护人民和国家的利益，这样的将帅，才是国家的宝贵财富。

战势不过奇正

In military tactics, there are only two types of operation: qi (unusual and unexpected attack) and zheng (normal and regular advance).

孙子说

战势不过奇正，奇正之变，不可胜穷也。

《孙子·兵势篇》

In military tactics, there are only two types of operation: qi (unusual and unexpected attack) and zheng (normal and regular advance). Yet their variations are limitless.

【注释】

势：态势。《孙子·始计篇》："计利以听，乃为之势，以佐其外。"**变**：变化，改变。《易·系辞下》："易穷则变，变则通，通则久。"

【译文】

战势不过是正面交锋和设计奇袭两种，而这两种战术的变化组合，却是不可穷尽的。

支形者，敌虽利我，我无出也

On the kind of terrain zhi which is disadvantageous to both sides, even if the enemy tempts you, you must not take the bait, but should withdraw.

支形者，敌虽利我，我无出也，引而去之，令敌半出而击之，利。

《孙子·地形篇》

On the kind of terrain zhi which is disadvantageous to both sides, even if the enemy tempts you, you must not take the bait, but should withdraw. Having lured the enemy halfway out, you can then strike to your advantage.

【注释】

支形：孙子把不利双方出击的地域叫做"支"。《孙子·地形篇》："我出而不利，彼出而不利，曰支。"利：利益。《商君书·算地》："利出于地，则民尽力。"引申为引诱。半出：出击一半时。

【译文】

在支形地域作战，纵然敌人引诱，也不可出击；可引兵离去，诱使敌人出击追赶，待敌人出一半时，我军突然回击，可取得胜利。

知彼知己，胜乃不殆

Know your enemy and know yourself，and victory will not be in question. . .

孙子说

知彼知己，胜乃不殆；知天知地，胜乃可全。

《孙子·地形篇》

Know your enemy and know yourself, and victory will not be in question; know both Heaven and Earth, and victory will be complete.

【注释】

知彼知己：对对方（多指敌人）和自己的情况都很了解。彼，对方。殆：危险，失败。知天知地：懂得利用天时地利。可全：可以保全。

【译文】

对敌我双方的情况都很了解，争取胜利不会失败；懂得利用天时地利，胜利就万无一失。

知彼知己，百战不殆

Know your enemy and know yourself, and you can fight a hundred battles without peril.

知彼知己，百战不殆。

《孙子·谋攻篇》

Know your enemy and know yourself, and you can fight a hundred battles without peril.

【注释】

　　知彼知己：深知敌我双方的情况。成语"知彼知己"出于此。**殆**（dài）：危险，失败。《老子》："知足不辱，知止不殆。"

【译文】

　　既了解敌人又了解自己，每战都不会有失败的危险。

189

知兵之将，民之司命

The commander who knows how to conduct a war is the arbiter of the people's fate. . .

知兵之将，民之司命，国家安危之主也。

《孙子·作战篇》

The commander who knows how to conduct a war is the arbiter of the people's fate, the man on whom the nation's security depends.

【注释】

司命：星名，传说主宰生死，引申为命运的主宰。**国家安危之主**：国家安危存亡的主宰者。主，主宰之意。

【译文】

懂得用兵的将领，掌握着百姓的生死存亡，主宰着国家的兴衰安危。

知兵者，动而不迷

Those who are well versed in warfare are never bewildered when they take action...

知兵者，动而不迷，举而不穷。

《孙子·地形篇》

Those who are well versed in warfare are never bewildered when they take action, and their resourcefulness in overcoming the enemy is limitless.

【注释】

动而不迷： 动，行动，指攻击敌人。不迷，不迷惑。因为决定攻击敌人的目的明确，所以才不会迷惑。**举而不穷：** 举，行动，举动。《左传·庄公二三年》："君举必书，书而不法，后嗣何观？" 穷，困厄。《论语·卫灵公》："君子亦有穷乎？"

【译文】

真正懂得用兵的人，他行动起来目的明确而不会迷惑，他采取措施变化无穷而不呆版。

知可以战与不可以战者胜

The side which knows when to fight and when not to will win. . . .

知可以战与不可以战者胜，识众寡之用者胜，上下同欲者胜，以虞待不虞者胜，将能而君不御者胜。

《孙子·谋攻篇》

The side which knows when to fight and when not to will win; the side which knows the difference between commanding a large army and commanding a small army will win; the side which has unity of purpose among its officers and men will win; the side which engages enemy troops that are unprepared with preparedness on its own part will win; and the side which has a capable commander who is free from interference from the king will win.

【注释】

以虞待不虞者胜：自己有准备对付没有准备之敌则能取胜。虞，意料，准备。《孟子·离娄上》："有不虞之誉，有求全之毁。"不虞，事前不考虑，无准备。

【译文】

知道什么情况下可以用兵什么情况下不可以用兵的人，能够取胜；明白敌我力量对比而能采用不同战术的人可以取胜；全军上下同心协力的可以取胜；有准备的军队对无准备的军队可以取胜；将帅有指挥才能而国君又不加掣肘的能够取胜。

智将务食于敌

A wise general does his best to feed his troops on the enemy's grain.

老人家说系列丛书

孙子说

智将务食于敌，食敌一钟，当吾二十钟，萁秆一石，当吾二十石。

《孙子·作战篇》

A wise general does his best to feed his troops on the enemy's grain, for one zhong[1,000 litres] of grain obtained from enemy territory is equivalent to 20 zhong carried from the home country, and one dan[60 kilos] of fodder from enemy territory is equivalent to 20 dan carried from the home country.

【注释】

智将：多谋善断的将领。《吴子·论将》："观敌之来，一坐一起，其政以理，其追北佯为不及，其见利佯为不知，如此将者，名为智将，勿与战矣。"**食于敌**：在敌国补充粮食。**钟**：古代容量单位。十釜为一钟。**萁（jì）秆**：豆秸，饲料。

【译文】

多谋善断的将领，一定会在敌国补充给养，吃掉敌国一钟粮食，就相当于从本国运来二十钟粮食；牲口吃掉敌国一石饲料，相当于从本国运来二十石饲料。

197

智者之虑，必杂于利害

In his deliberations, the wise commander will take into account both the favorable and the unfavorable factors.

智者之虑，必杂于利害。

《孙子·九变篇》

In his deliberations, the wise commander will take into account both the favorable and the unfavorable factors.

【注释】

杂于利害：兼顾到利与害两个方面。杂，俱。引申为兼顾。

孙子认为"杂于利，而务可信也；杂于害，而患可解也"。

【译文】

聪明统帅考虑问题，总是兼顾到利和害两个方面。

主不可以怒而兴师

The king should not start a war simply out of anger...

主不可以怒而兴师，将不可愠而致战。

《孙子·火攻篇》

The king should not start a war simply out of anger; the commander should not fight a battle simply out of resentment.

【注释】

愠：恼怒，怨愤。

孙子认为英明的国君对战争要慎重考虑，不能凭一时怒气而兴师动众。优秀的将帅对战争也要警惕，不能因一时怒气而对敌作战，这是安定国家，保全军队的根本原则。

【译文】

国君切不可因一时恼怒而兴兵，将帅不可因一时愤恨而交战。

图书在版编目（CIP）数据

孙子说 / 蔡希勤编注 . —北京：华语教学出版社， 2006
　　（中国圣人文化丛书 . 老人家说系列）
ISBN 978-7-80200-214-2

Ⅰ. 孙… Ⅱ. 蔡… Ⅲ. 汉语—对外汉语教学—语言读物 Ⅳ.H195.5

中国版本图书馆 CIP 数据核字（2006）第 071755 号

出版人：单　瑛
责任编辑：韩　晖　　封面设计：胡　湖
印刷监制：佟汉冬　　绘　　图：李士伋

老人家说·孙子说

蔡希勤　编注

＊

© 华语教学出版社
华语教学出版社出版
（中国北京百万庄大街 24 号　邮政编码 100037）
电话：(86)10-68320585
传真：(86)10-68326333
网址：www.sinolingua.com.cn
电子信箱：hyjx@ sinolingua.com.cn
北京松源印刷有限公司印刷
中国国际图书贸易总公司海外发行
（中国北京车公庄西路 35 号）
北京邮政信箱第 399 号　邮政编码 100044
新华书店国内发行
2006 年（32 开）第一版
2007 年第一版第二次印刷
2009 年第一版第三次印刷
（汉英）
ISBN 978-7-80200-214-2
9-CE-3731P
定价：29.80 元